W9-CHP-634

11/10/18

Nancy

My prayer for you, my friend,
is that you always remember a truth that's
as old as time itself…
all things are possible when you believe…
and may you know without a doubt
that you are worthy, you are deserving,
and you are loved.

*Thanks for being
my friend,*

Andrea

Copyright © 2016 by PrimaDonna Entertainment Corp.
Copyright © 2016 by Blue Mountain Arts, Inc.

ISBN: 978-1-68088-071-7

Printed in China.
First Printing: 2016

Blue Mountain Arts, Inc.
P.O. Box 4549, Boulder, Colorado 80306

My Prayer for You, My Friend

Wishes, Hopes, and
Words of Encouragement for
Someone Special

Donna Fargo

Blue Mountain Press™
Boulder, Colorado

My Prayer for You, My Friend

When I think about the people who are
    important to me,
who are often in my thoughts and prayers,
    I think of you.
The prayer doesn't change much.
It always starts with wishing you health
    and happiness
and asking God to take good care of you.

I pray that hope and faith are your constant
    companions and that the gift of love inside
your heart will help you do amazing things.
Even when you're discouraged
    and life is not fair,
I hope that you never let anything steal your joy,
that you celebrate the miracle of each moment,
and count your blessings every day.

As you embrace every new challenge,
my prayer is that you'll do your best
    and not worry about the rest —
that you'll change what you need to
    and accept what you can't change.
I believe in you, and
I believe that your future will be secure,
success will follow you,
and you will fulfill your potential.

My prayer for you, my friend,
is that you always remember a truth that's
as old as time itself...
all things are possible when you believe...
and may you know without a doubt
that you are worthy, you are deserving,
and you are loved.

Your Friendship Is One of My Greatest Treasures

Friendship is one of those big things like love and happiness. It's so necessary that the heart is not satisfied without it. True friends make us feel like our lives matter. They are there for us when others may not be, and they reassure us that we belong somewhere in this big sea of people.

You are a true friend to me. Whether you know it or not, the contributions you have made to nurture my dreams and wishes for my future have been an ever-present force. Thank you for being on my side. You treat me right all the time, and I appreciate you so much.

I am inspired by the way you wrap your arms around life and make a difference in someone else's day. In you, I see someone who doesn't just talk the talk but also walks the walk. Your words and actions tell the truth of who you are. You turn disappointments into triumphs. You're a survivor and a wonderful example.

Regardless of how often we communicate or whether we're near or far apart, please know how much I value our relationship. Your friendship is such a great treasure, and I'm so fortunate to have you for a friend.

I Ask God to Take Good Care of You

I ask God to... reward you with a strong faith for your efforts and be with you through any challenges and adjustments you may face. I ask Him to restore you when you're not yourself, replace your doubts and fears with assurance and certainty, and show you the way to realize your unlimited potential.

I ask God to... give you peace when you're conflicted, answers when you have questions, and clarity and direction when you need special guidance. May you have unwavering determination when you need not only knowledge but also wisdom in your search for truth. May you have company when you're lonely and you just need a friend.

Whatever puts the twinkle in your eye, the melody in your heart song, the sunny in your sky... that's what I ask God for you.

Whatever gives you endless opportunities, brings you meaningful experiences, allows you to recall the sweetest memories, and makes you thankful for your blessings... these are the things I ask for you.

Whatever you need to find solutions to your problems, well-being for your body, satisfaction in your soul, and delight in each new day... I ask all these things for you.

What more could I ask for you?

I ask that you drink from the cup of life with gratitude and make every day a great day to be alive.

Blessings May Be Angels in Disguise

If the path ahead of you ever turns dark, look for a special angel to light the way. There may be an odd coincidence, a friend who shows up unexpectedly, or something wonderful that you can't put into words or understand. This is often an answer to your prayer.

We all have guardian angels who can turn our tears into smiles and carry us on their wings when ours are broken. They can instill in us the courage and strength to move some of the mountains in our way. They can caution us and save us from negative consequences. They can throw us a life raft when we need one and pull us to safety without our even knowing it. Sometimes they sit on our shoulders and whisper encouraging thoughts or words to fit a particular circumstance. Be thankful for these blessings. You may unknowingly be entertaining your angel.

The power of spiritual energy is amazing. We are told that we have angels sent to minister to us. Some believe that angels bring messages straight from God. The Bible says God will give His angels charge over us to guard us in all ways — to guide, comfort, and provide for us. Imagine how special we are to God that He would give each one of us our very own angel.

As You Travel the Road of Life…

I wish you a good map to where you want to go. I wish you good luck through all the detours. I wish you a clear mind, a strong will, and wisdom in every decision you make. I wish you enough confidence in yourself to make whatever changes you may need to.

May you have a close walk with God and realize that you're more than your body and mind; may you also know the power of your spirit. May you find a beautiful rainbow through every trial and storm you face. Just as the rain waters the flowers to make them grow, may you bloom big through the tears that cause you pain — and may you learn the lessons they can teach you.

May you realize that you are the co-creator of your destiny. Life is a journey full of twists and turns. Stay true to your purpose. Love and allow yourself to be loved. Remember that every action has a consequence. Be courageous, but also be cautious and wise. Let your conscience guide you to act in the highest and noblest manner, and remember that practicing the Golden Rule will always lead you in the right direction on the road of life.

Have Some Fun!

Loosen up
Kick up your feet
Have a little fun every day
Each moment doesn't have to be
So busy or so serious
That you can't also take time
    to play

Let yourself party
Every now and then
Do what you really want to do
It's an honorable thing
To be good to others
But don't forget to be good
    to you too

If you're worrying too much
Or you're just bored with life
Don't underestimate the
    importance of fun

Celebrate every day
No matter what
Let your light shine
    as bright as the sun

Throw out the schedule
Get rid of the rules
Be as free as a bird in the sky
Let yourself dream big
See yourself "getting there"
Catch a ride on a cloud and
    fly high

Roll in the green grass
Act like a little child
Let go of any troubles
    and strife
Make every day a holiday
And every day a great day
After all, this is your life!

Believe in Yourself

I believe all of us have a built-in compass to help us get to wherever we desire to go. Don't forget to trust that compass and refer to it often, for with that trusting will come the strength to bear whatever life deals you.

Don't get led astray. Ask your heart for the truth, and you will come up with the answer and the good judgment to make the decisions you'll need to make. Love everyone, and don't question love's reception. Do the best you can. Live each day as it comes. We can't get ahead of ourselves anyway.

Remember: while you may have questions now, somewhere inside you and later on, there will be better answers and workable solutions. It takes patience and a strong will to get through life's changes when you're trying to reach goals, solve problems, and make dreams come true. Though at times the difficulties may seem insurmountable, I know you are strong and you can handle whatever comes your way. Believe in yourself.

When You Don't Know What to Do... Pray About It

When you don't know what to do,
which way to turn, or on whom to rely...
When you can't decide whether
one action would be better than another...
When you're anxious and confused
and your heart and mind are in conflict...
Don't forget to pray about it.

Pray for results too.
Prayer is our direct spiritual line to God.
Prayer will bring you peace
and cause you to rest your case.
It will keep you humble and
make you feel better and
strengthen your relationship with God.

Remember that God is love.
He is faithful and He is good, and He
wants you to have whatever you desire.
Pray about everything
that concerns you...
and believe that your prayer
is answered.
Then refuse to worry about it anymore.
It's settled.

I Promise You This...

Acceptance... without judgment.
Prayers... when you need them.
Understanding... when you're conflicted.
Loyalty... all the time.
Friendship... forever.

When you're feeling low... I'll try to lift
    you up.
When you're on top of the world...
    I'll celebrate with you.
When you're lost... I'll try to find you.
When you're confused... I'll try to help you.
If you want company... call me.
When you need me... I'll be there —
    you can count on it.

I'll laugh with you and cry with you.
I'll be by your side and wish the best for you.
This is a no-strings-attached kind of caring.
You don't need to do anything
    to win my friendship.
You have it.

Because of your example,
I have learned that a positive anything
is better than any negative whatever
and that we have the power to choose
    our attitude.
You have shown me that our friendship
    is a two-way street
and we're in this for the long run.
You have taught me many valuable lessons,
and my life is so much richer because of you.
You are one of my favorite people
    on the planet,
and that is one thing that will never change.

I Would If I Could

If I could capture the beauty of a spring flower and the sunshine in a baby's smile and mix them with a call from someone you'd like to hear from... I'd give them all to you to make your day.

If there could be an absence of anything that would bring you down... if every person you love could make you feel loved back... if whatever you wish for most could miraculously be supplied... this is what I would give you if I could.

If you could see your life with all its essence
and be at peace no matter what... if you could
approve of yourself without censure and live with
no regrets, I would supply you with whatever it
would take to make it so... if I could.

Of course, I can't do any of that, but I can remind
you just how special you really are and encourage
you to follow your heart wherever it leads. That's
what I can do... and will keep on doing!

There Is Nothing So Precious as a Friend

When we find a friend, especially one whose friendship grows over time, the feeling of emotional trust and support we get is amazing. From that good fortune, a "happy" light goes on inside us. It's like we've found someone important who's been missing — an advocate, an ally, and a favorite person who really matters to us.

There's a beautiful combination of energy and comfort. It's a calming feeling. We are more at home in the world. We're not so afraid. We all need this exchange of camaraderie and goodwill. Friendship empowers us and makes us feel that we're okay and we have someone to care for who also cares for us.

When we have problems, our friend may be the only person we call. We know that we'll be taken seriously and we'll be treated with compassion, respect, and empathy. We will have someone who's there for us through the hard places and who will celebrate every victory with us. We know we can depend on this person to walk in our shoes and share our hurts as much as possible. And we will return that same kind of friendship without question.

Like the beloved perennials that create the most beautiful gardens, there is nothing so precious as a friend to the landscape of our lives.

You are that precious friend to me.

We Share a Special Connection

You are honest with me — you trust me and you care about my welfare. You allow me to know your weaknesses, just as I let you know mine.

You are interested in what I am saying and what I'm concerned about, and you think back on our conversations when I am not around in an effort to find answers to things you know I question.

You share my worries and can tell when I need a hand to pick up the pieces and move on. You are also sensitive to my insecurities. We inform each other about what is happening in our lives so that we can be better friends. We have a real connection, and loyalty is our bond.

In other words, we are on each other's side... to really listen and not just wait to talk. The friendship we enjoy makes me feel more secure and valued.

You're there, always there. You don't give up on me when I disappoint you. Thank you for that, most of all.

You're not just anyone to me. You're my friend. I think God made you extra special. And I believe our friendship is destined to stand the tests of time and change.

We'll Always Be Friends

There's a genuineness between us that survives through troubles and trials and upsets because we know each other's values, feelings, and views, and we treat each other the way we want to be treated.

We honor our friendship by being available, showing up, and voluntarily going out of our way. Time and experience have taught us that we can depend on each other. We take turns with our complaining and sense when the other one is seriously troubled or just "venting." We call each other to clear our minds, to let go and lighten up, and to share pain, happiness, and sadness.

When our habits and ways seem to be set in concrete
and we sabotage ourselves for whatever reasons,
we remind each other that it's time to try a different
approach. Whether we succeed or fail at something we're
trying to change, our sincere desire to help each other
provides the therapy we need to move on. We both know
that giving up is a choice — just as embracing the saving
grace of hope is — and that together we can get through
any storm.

We always encourage each other, and we show our
friendship by our actions, not just our words. Because
we really care, we do all we can to support each other's
efforts and aspirations. We forgive quickly when there's
a conflict, and we treat each other with respect. We are
allies and dream sharers and life travelers who know that
friendship is one of the greatest gifts we can have and
that ours will last forever.

Thank You for Everything

For those times I've missed saying "thank you," I want to thank you now for being a soft and gentle light in my life.

Thank you for the thoughtfulness you've shown to me so many times. Thank you for all the things you've done for me... not out of obligation, but in the spirit of love and concern for my happiness and well-being. Because of your faith in me, I have more faith in myself.

Thank you for the lessons in humanity that I have learned from you. You accept others as they are; you build bridges and not walls. Thank you for being such a beautiful example of a caring person.

We need people in our lives we can share our everyday thoughts with and live together in peace and harmony as we grow old. We need give-and-take relationships so we will know there are people we can trust and who trust us and with whom we share a lasting commitment.

We all need someone we can depend on. You have been that someone for me, and you are a gift to my heart.

I know I've said it before, but it is worthy of repetition… I appreciate you, and I wish you the best. Thank you for everything.

I'm So Lucky to Have You for a Friend

As friends, you've never tried to change me, and I've never tried to change you. We know each other's best and not-so-best sides. We've called it like it was and like it wasn't. And each of us would probably admit that we've made our fair share of what seemed to be less-than-perfect moves. We've trudged through some serious stuff and kept each other steady when we were being bumped around on some rough roads.

We've kept our sense of humor when the situation wasn't the least bit funny. We've done our share of hurting but always managed to carry on regardless of how we felt or how rocky the ride was.

You make me feel special because you often go out of your way for me. You mean what you say and say what you mean. You'll do whatever it takes for someone if you think it's the right thing to do. You're not afraid to admit when you are wrong. You are willing to learn something new — to grow, to fail, to succeed, and to take chances. I love these qualities in you; they set you apart from others. You're different, you're rare… and I hope you never change.

I just want you to hear this from me: my world is better with you in it, my life is happier because you share it, and I'm so glad I have you for a friend.

Good Friends Live in Each Other's Heart

Good friends walk through life together, whether they live close or far apart. They know that the other one is there... to share the highs and the lows and everything else.

Good friends are connected at the heart, and their dedication to their friendship is permanent. They look out for each other, and they can talk about things they may not even discuss with their families. Each of them knows the other will understand, no matter what.

Good friends aren't afraid to break the rules, defend each other, and go out of their way. They're together through the good times and the bad. Their loyalty is strong and lasting, and their choice to be each other's friend is clear and absolute. They know that they'll keep on being there through everything life has in store for them.

No one can take the place of a good friend, just like no one can take your place with me. You will always live in my heart.

I Wish You Happiness

I wish you little things, like a warm shoulder
　　to lean on when the world seems cold...
the feeling you get from falling snow or a
　　walk on the beach...
confidence when you're uneasy and your
　　self-esteem is low...
opportunities when you think they're
　　out of reach.

I wish you little things, like a kind word when
　　you're afraid and you need direction...
a friendly smile and a helpful hand when
　　life is hard...
fun times and laughter to fill the silence and
　　put your troubles in perspective...
signs of hope when you think you've played
　　your last card.

And I wish you big things, too, like perfect
    health in your body, mind, and soul...
someone to love and be loved by, good friends,
    and personal success...
unconditional acceptance and forgiveness
    when you need it most...
closeness with God, prosperity, and happiness.

In short, I wish everything good for you, and
    one more thing...
I hope you soar like a fearless eagle
    and shine like the brightest star
as you maneuver through the life storms that
    come along.
I pray for your every wish to be granted
    and your every dream to come true...
and may the sweetest melodies you've ever heard
    make up the soundtrack of your life song.

You Are Always in My Prayers

I believe there are no requests that go unheard, no doubts that can't be turned into faith, and no hurts that can't be healed, so I send these thoughts and prayers for you up to the heavens...

I pray that you are happy and that you're experiencing the full extent of your potential. I ask God to help you to do the things you want to do... to accomplish your goals, find answers to your questions, and live according to your purpose in life.

I pray that you are blessed with good health and that you stay that way. I know that your joyful outlook and positive attitude will serve you well.

As your friend, you have my steadfast agreement that any problems that present themselves will be successfully resolved. Individually, we are strong in faith, but together, we are stronger.

My prayer is that you are managing your everyday life to your satisfaction and that you have the financial security and material needs you desire. I hope you are emboldened and inspired by an ever-growing faith and that you feel loved and appreciated by those you care about.

I need some new words to tell you how thankful I am to have you for a friend. I just hope our friendship is as much of a support system for you as it is for me. You're one of God's works of art, and you're one of a kind to me. May God keep you safe and strong, fill you with awesome wonder, and bless you in everything you do.

About the Author

With her first album, *The Happiest Girl in the Whole U.S.A.*, which achieved platinum status and earned her a Grammy, Donna Fargo established herself as an award-winning singer, songwriter, and performer. Her credits include seven Academy of Country Music awards, five Billboard awards, fifteen Broadcast Music Incorporated (BMI) writing awards, and two National Association of Recording Merchandisers awards for best-selling artist. She has also been honored by the Country Music Association, the National Academy of Recording Arts and Sciences, and the Music Operators of America, and she was the first inductee into the North America Country Music Associations, International's Hall of Fame. As a writer, her most coveted awards, in addition to the Robert J. Burton Award that she won for "Most Performed Song of the Year," are her Million-Air Awards, presented to writers of songs that achieve the blockbuster status of one million or more performances. In 2009, the state of North Carolina named a highway after her, and in 2010, she was inducted into the North Carolina Music Hall of Fame.

Prior to achieving superstardom and becoming one of the most prolific songwriters in Nashville, Donna was a high school English teacher. It was her love of the English language and her desire to communicate sincere and honest emotions that compelled Donna to try her hand at writing something other than song lyrics. Donna is also the author of *My Prayer for You*, and her writings appear on Blue Mountain Arts greeting cards, calendars, and other gift items.